DANGEROUS & DEADLY
TOXIC ANIMALS

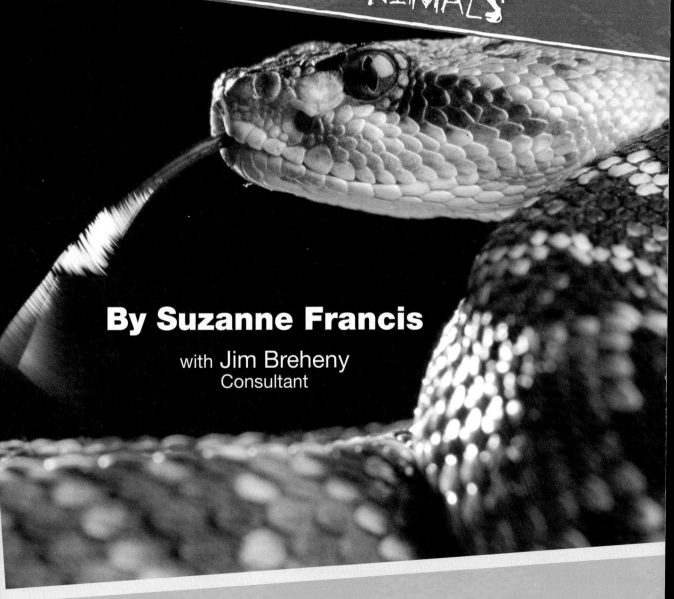

By Suzanne Francis

with **Jim Breheny**
Consultant

Scholastic Inc.

New York • Toronto • London • Auckland • Sydney
Mexico City • New Delhi • Hong Kong • Buenos Aires

ISBN-13: 978-0-439-02571-3
ISBN-10: 0-439-02571-0

Design by Aruna Goldstein
All Mac the veiled chameleon illustrations by James Elston

Photo Credits:
Cover and title page: (Black-tailed rattlesnake) © Dag Sundberg/The Image Bank/Getty Images. Back cover: (Jumping spider) © Seet/Shutterstock.com. Page 3: (Scorpion) © Photos.com (RF). Pages 4–5: (Rattlesnake) © Joel Sartore/National Geographic/Getty Images. Pages 6–7: (Chameleon) © Mike Severns/Stone/Getty Images. Page 8: (Poison dart frog) © Art Wolfe/Photo Researchers, Inc. Page 9: (Redback spider) © 2006 Getty Images. Pages 10–11: (Scorpion) © Photos.com (RF); (scorpion eating grasshopper) © Anthony Bannister/NHPA. Page 12: (Scorpion with babies) © Photos.com (RF). Page 13: (Deathstalker scorpion) © Stephen Dalton/Photo Researchers, Inc.; (emperor scorpion) © David Aubrey/Photo Researchers, Inc. Pages 14–15: (Yellow–lined pit viper) © George Grall/National Geographic/Getty Images; (pit viper baring fangs) © Carsten Peter/National Geographic/Getty Images. Page 16: (Viper eating rodent) © David A. Northcott/CORBIS. Page 17: (Banded sea krait) © Gregory Ochocki/Photo Researchers, Inc. Pages 18–19: (Gaboon viper) © E. R. Degginger/Photo Researchers, Inc.; (inland taipan) © B. G. Thomson/Photo Researchers, Inc.; (spitting cobra) © Digital Vision/ Getty Images; (western diamondback rattlesnake) © Alan and Sandy Carey/Photo Researchers, Inc.; (black mamba) © Rod Patterson/Gallo Images/Getty Images. Pages 20–21: (Jumping spider with caterpillar) © George Grall/National Geographic/Getty Images; (black and yellow garden spider) © Millard H. Sharp/Photo Researchers, Inc.; (black widow) © Scott Camazine/Photo Researchers, Inc.; (funnel-web spider) © B. G. Thomson/Photo Researchers, Inc. Page 22: (Snake being milked for venom) © Jeffrey L. Rotman/CORBIS. Page 23: (Poison dart frog) © Art Wolfe/Photo Researchers, Inc. Page 24: (Gila monster) © Tim Flach/Stone/Getty Images; (puss caterpillar) © Robert Noonan/Photo Researchers, Inc. Page 25: (Coral snake) © Karl H. Switak/ Photo Reseachers, Inc.; (milk snake) © Martin Harvey/NHPA. Pages 26–27: (Box jelly) © David Doubilet/National Geographic/Getty Images; (nematocyst) © Dr. Dennis Kunkel/Visuals Unlimited/Getty Images. Page 28: (Blue-ringed octopus) © Gary Bell/Taxi/Getty Images; (stonefish) © B. Jones & M. Shimlock/NHPA. Page 29: (Lionfish) © David Nardini/Taxi/Getty Images. Page 30: (Spiny puffer fish) © Steven Hunt/The Image Bank/Getty Images. Page 31: (Bill Holmstrom) © Julie Larsen Maher/WCS. Page 32: (Green lynx spider) © Byron Jorjorian/Stone/ Getty Images.

TABLE OF CONTENTS

Scorpion

WELCOME TO 3-D ANIMALS IN ACTION!

▷ Mac
Veiled chameleon

Hey there and welcome to *3-D Animals in Action*! My name's Mac and I'll be hanging out with you on your action-packed travels through the wacky and wild world of animals. We're going to take a look at a bunch of critters that most people stay away from: **venomous** and **poisonous animals**. Yup, we're going to get up close and personal with the world's deadliest and most dangerous creatures. Did you know that...

- The most venomous animal in the world is practically invisible?

- There's a frog with a poison so powerful that one drop can kill several people?

- Some kinds of snakes can spit their venom up to 6 feet (2 m) away?

Pretty cool, huh? We'll also find the answers to questions like:

- What's the difference between a venomous animal and a poisonous one?

- Which snake is the deadliest?

- How do doctors treat people with a venomous animal bite?

4

A rattlesnake shows its fangs.

This is one Awesome Adventure you don't want to miss! Turn the page and let's get going!

WACKY AND WILD IN 3-D!

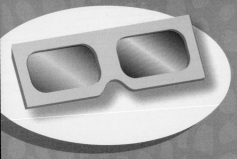

Your *3-D Animals in Action* book comes with a pair of awesome **3-D glasses** that aren't just for show. Check out the picture on the next page without your glasses—just a regular ol' reptile, right? Now, put on those glasses. Notice anything different?

Keep your glasses handy when you're reading this book. Whenever you see the **3-D icon** above, put on your glasses for some in-your-face animal action!

You'll also see some other **symbols** as you read. Here's what they are and how they'll help you on your adventures.

The Word Bird will explain some tricky words that you might find in this book. If you find a word that you don't know, look for this bird to give you the scoop.

When you see **That's Wild!**, get ready for info on something extraordinary!

Love animal jokes? Have a good chuckle with **Critter Crack-Ups!**

A chameleon catches a snack.

TOTALLY TOXIC

Not all deadly and dangerous creatures are the same. Did you know that there's a difference between a venomous animal and a poisonous one? Check out these pages to learn the difference between these totally toxic animals.

Poison dart frog

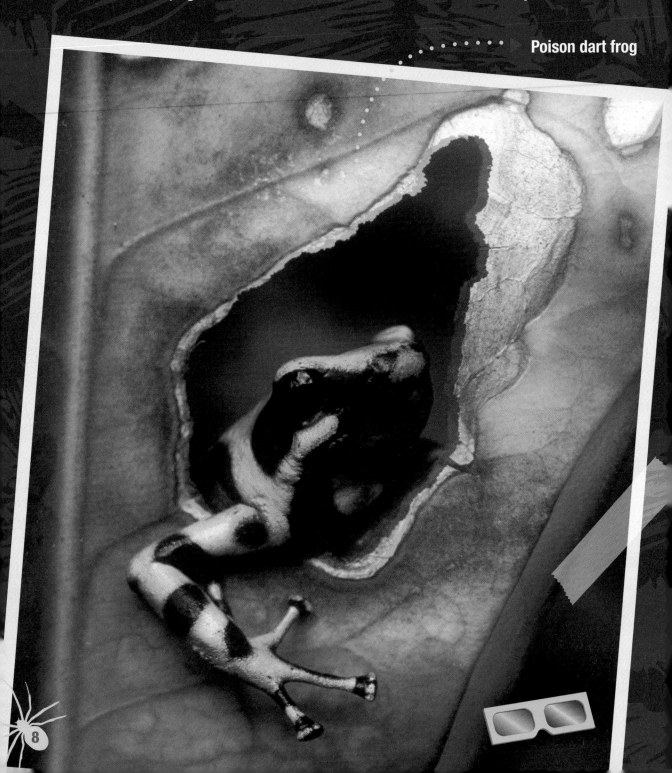

A venomous redback spider

The Word Bird

A *toxin* is a chemical made by a plant or animal that can make another animal sick, or even kill it.

Very Venomous

Both venomous and poisonous animals have **toxins** (TOK-sins) in their venom or poison that they use to catch food or to protect themselves. **Venomous animals** have **special body parts** like fangs or stingers to **inject venom** into another animal. But these critters don't just go around stinging or biting things just for kicks! Most of them need that venom to help them **catch food.** If a venomous animal feels threatened, it can also use its venom to protect itself.

Pretty Poisonous

Unlike a venomous animal, a **poisonous animal** doesn't have stingers or special teeth to deliver its toxins. Instead, its toxins are **distributed throughout its body or on its skin** to help the animal **protect** itself. In other words, poisonous animals don't use toxins to catch food! Another animal has to touch or eat a poisonous animal to get sick. Usually a poisonous animal's toxins make it taste terrible, so a predator looking for a tasty snack spits it right out.

that's Wild! Many toxic animals are brightly colored to let other animals know that eating them might be their last meal! For more on animal colors, turn to page 25.

SUPER SCORPIONS

The first group of venomous animals that we're going to meet have been walking the Earth for 430 million years and live all over the world. They've even been found under snow-covered rocks in the Himalayas!

*That's one **cool** hiding place!*

What are these amazing animals? They're **scorpions** (SKOR-pee-uhns)! Check out the list below to learn everything you need to know about these awesome animals.

The Word Bird

An *invertebrate* is any animal without a backbone.

★ Believe it or not, scorpions are **arachnids** (uh-RACK-nids), which is a group of **invertebrates** (in-VUR-tuh-brits) that include spiders. And just like spiders, scorpions have **eight legs** to get around on.

★ Along with eight legs, a scorpion has two big **pincers** that help grab prey and hold on while it stings.

★ A scorpion's body has **12 segments**, or sections, which are covered in a **tough outer shell**. Some places on the body have **hair-like bristles** that pick up vibrations to help the scorpion find prey like insects, spiders, and centipedes.

★ The last six segments of a scorpion's body make up its **tail**. The very last segment has two **venom glands** and a sharp, curved **stinger**. Yow!

★ Scorpions have **bad eyesight**, but that doesn't stop them from being expert hunters! Since they're **active at night**, scorpions hunt in the dark and use their other senses to help them nab a meal.

▲ **Last segment of tail has two venom glands and a stinger**

Eight legs for walking ▼

Stinger Zinger

Once a scorpion senses prey is near, it chases it down and grabs it with its pincers. If the prey doesn't give in easily, the scorpion curls its tail over its back at lightning speed and stings the animal to inject its venom. Most scorpions have venom that paralyzes the prey so the scorpion can chow down.

A scorpion eats a grasshopper.

▼ Body has 12 segments

▼ Two pincers to grab prey

Critter Crack-Ups

Q: Why do scorpions make good pals?
A: Because they help out in a *pinch*.

Pinch Me

Are big scorpions with big pincers the most venomous? Think again! It's the smaller scorpions that pack the most punch. Big scorpions with big pincers have the muscle to hang on to prey, so they don't need their venom to be super-strong. Scorpions with smaller pincers need something extra to catch their supper, so they have powerful venom to knock prey out.

that's Wild! Scorpions are the only arachnids that give birth to live babies. And get a load of this—when the little scorpions are born, they climb onto their mother's back and hang out! But this free ride only lasts until they *molt*, or shed their skin for the first time.

The Ouch Factor

Like most animals, scorpions use their venom to defend themselves if they have to, but they're more likely to run away and hide first. In fact, most people who are stung by scorpions accidentally step on them as they're putting on their shoes, since a shoe seems like a great hiding place to a scorpion.

Might be a little **smelly**, though!

But being stung by a scorpion isn't usually deadly. There are over 1,000 different kinds of scorpions, but only about 25 have venom that can kill humans. If people see a doctor after being stung, they're usually fine.

▶ **A scorpion mom carries her babies on her back.**

scorpion superstars

So now that you know a bit about scorpions, are you ready to meet a few? Check out these two superstars below.

Emperor Scorpion
Size: Grows up to 8 inches (20 cm) long
Location: Africa

The **emperor scorpion** is one of the largest scorpions out there. With its black body and big pincers, the emperor scorpion looks fierce, but it's actually pretty peaceful. Since this critter has mild venom and only *looks* bad to the bone, the emperor scorpion is the top pick for movies and TV shows that need a scorpion or two (or a few hundred!). In the wild, the emperor scorpion uses its legs to dig into termite mounds. Once inside, it hangs out, since there's plenty of its favorite food—termites!

Deathstalker Scorpion
Size: Grows up to 4½ inches (11 cm) long
Location: Northern Africa, Middle East

Sometimes called the yellow scorpion or the Israeli desert scorpion, the **deathstalker scorpion** is the most venomous scorpion in the world. Deathstalker stings are very serious, and a handful of people die every year after being stung. But here's a neat fact: Although their venom is deadly, scientists study deathstalkers because chemicals in their venom may help people with a certain kind of brain cancer.

SNAKES ALIVE!

Just like scorpions, our second group of venomous animals lives just about everywhere—in deserts, forests, trees, and even in water! And there are about 3,000 different kinds alive today. What are they? They're **snakes**! Check out these pages and learn more about these scaly slitherers.

- ✮ Snakes are **reptiles**, so they're in the same group with animals like lizards, turtles, and crocodiles. Like all reptiles, snakes are **cold-blooded**.

- ✮ All snakes are carnivores and are either **constrictors** or are **venomous**. Constrictors get food by catching prey and squeezing their bodies to kill them. Venomous snakes catch their prey by biting and injecting them with venom.

- ✮ Venomous snakes have special teeth called **fangs** that are **grooved** or **hollow with small openings at the ends**. The teeth are connected to **glands** under a snake's eyes that make venom. When the snake bites its prey, venom flows through the fangs and is injected into the prey.

- ✮ Snakes have very **flexible skulls** with **special jaws**. These jaws allow them to swallow prey that's way bigger than their heads—whole!

The Word Bird

If an animal is *cold-blooded*, its body temperature changes with its environment. It sits in the sun to warm up or parks it in the shade to cool off. *Warm-blooded* animals can control their own body temperature.

▶ Yellow-lined pit viper

14

Ssssensational Senses

Some snakes have bad eyesight. So how do these snakes track down prey? They smell 'em out! A snake has a **special organ in its mouth** that works with its **tongue** to get the 411 on its surroundings. The snake sticks out its tongue and flicks it around to capture scents in the air. When the snake brings its tongue back into its mouth, this organ analyzes the scents and passes the info to the brain.

Boas, pythons, and pit vipers have another super-sense that helps them hunt. These snakes have special openings in the skin around their mouths called **heat pits**. Heat pits help snakes sense **tiny changes in temperature**—even the tiny change from a **warm-blooded** animal just being near them! The snake can figure out exactly where the prey is and strike, even in total darkness.

Heat pit

Fang

A venomous snake shows its fangs.

Venom Varieties

Snake venom is actually the snake's own **saliva**, or spit. What makes venom different than regular ol' spit is the toxins in it. Depending on where the snake lives and what kind of prey it's after, its venom can be more or less toxic. For example, a big land snake might have less toxic venom since it has an easier time holding on to prey, while a small snake that feeds on birds is more venomous so that its meal doesn't fly the coop. Some snakes even have special venom that will only affect certain kinds of animals, but not others.

Folding Fangs

A group of venomous snakes called vipers have **foldable fangs**. Vipers' fangs have a **hinge** that folds down when they close their mouths. But even if a venomous snake does bite its own tongue, no worries—venomous animals aren't affected by their own venom, so it doesn't hurt them.

that's Wild!

What happens if a snake's fang breaks off while it's on the prowl? Snakes have extra sets of fangs behind their main ones. So when a fang breaks off, a new fang moves forward and takes its place.

Striking Out

Once a snake scopes out its prey, it **stays very still** and waits for it to come near. Some snakes have **coloring** and **patterns** that make it hard to see them when they lie perfectly still, so an unsuspecting animal doesn't have a clue! Once the prey comes close, the snake **lunges** and **bites** it. Depending on how strong the snake's venom is, the snake might let the prey wander off while the venom does its work. Then the snake will track the knocked-out prey down with its super-senses. Or, if the snake's venom is powerful stuff, it might gulp its meal down right away.

A striped eyelash viper catches a rodent.

Banded sea krait

Shy Snakes

Snakes, like other venomous animals, don't seek out people. They're shy creatures and would prefer to slither away than come face-to-face with a gigantic animal…like you! A snake only bites a person when it's scared, so it's best to keep your distance and respect these super-cool critters.

Critter Crack-Ups

Q: What did the viper say after it caught its first meal?

A: Now I've got the *fang* of it!

Surf's Up!

Did you know that not all venomous snakes live on land? Yup, it's true! **Sea snakes** ride the waves in search of fish and other tasty seafood treats. Unlike their landlubber cousins, sea snakes have flat, paddle-like tails to help them swim, but they aren't very speedy. So to catch their fast-moving meals, these snakes have highly toxic venom and are more venomous than most land snakes. For a sea snake, it's important to have venom that can kill prey quickly. They need to catch that fast food before it swims away or sinks to the bottom of the ocean!

a scaly hall of fame

So now that you've brushed up on venomous snakes, check out the ones on these pages with some serious claims to fame.

Longest Fang

Name: Gaboon viper
Size: Up to 3 feet (1 m) long
Location: West and central Africa

Gaboon vipers have the longest fangs of any snake—up to 1½ inches (4 cm) long! Because it has a short and thick body, the gaboon viper isn't the kind of snake that puts up a chase. Using its skin patterns and coloring, it hides and waits for prey to come along before it strikes.

Most Venomous

Name: Inland taipan
Size: Up to 6 feet (2 m) long
Location: Central Australia

The **inland taipan** is considered the most venomous snake on Earth. One bite from this snake has enough venom to kill about 60 humans! Even though it's the most toxic snake around, it hasn't hurt many people. Since it lives in remote parts of Australia, folks don't bump into the inland taipan very often.

Super Squirter

Name: Spitting cobra
Size: Up to 5 feet (1½ m) long
Location: Asia and Africa

Spitting cobras have an extra funky feature: They can spray venom! Special muscles around the venom glands let these snakes squirt venom up to 6 feet (2 m) away! If cornered, these cobras spit venom right into their attacker's eyes. The venom isn't deadly when it gets in the eyes, but it's painful enough to let the snake make a quick getaway.

Most Musical

Name: Western diamondback rattlesnake
Size: Up to 6½ feet (2 m) long
Location: Southwestern United States

Rattlesnakes use a musical method to defend themselves. The tips of their tails have loose scales inside that act like beads. When the snake shakes the tip, the scales make a rattling noise. The world's biggest rattlesnake is the **western diamondback**. While its venom isn't very toxic, this snake injects large amounts of it, so its bites are considered very serious.

Speediest Snake

Name: Black mamba
Size: Up to 14 feet (4 m) long
Location: Africa

The **black mamba** is the fastest snake on Earth. It can catch speeds up to 12 miles (19 km) per hour! Along with being a speedy slitherer, black mamba venom is extremely deadly. Just two drops can kill a human—and this snake can hold up to 20 drops in its fangs!

Not-So-Sweet Spiders

Our third group of venomous animals are creepy, crawly critters that live just about everywhere, including your own backyard! They're **spiders**! Check out these pages to learn more about these backyard beasties.

* Like scorpions, spiders are **arachnids**. Like all arachnids, spiders have **eight walking legs**. The bottom of a spider's feet have **special oils** which help it walk on webs without getting stuck.

* All spiders are **venomous** and use their venom to knock out prey. Spiders have a pair of **fangs** to bite and inject venom. Most spiders' venom doesn't affect humans, but some spider bites can be dangerous.

* All spiders produce **silk**, which they might use to **spin webs**, **trap prey**, and **cover their eggs**. These silk threads are extremely strong—at the same size, spider silk is stronger than steel!

A jumping spider eats a caterpillar.

A garden spider in its web.

Check out two of the world's most venomous spiders below.

Black Widow

Size: Females can grow up to 1½ inches (4 cm) long, males only ¾ inches (2 cm) long
Location: North America

The **black widow** is the most venomous spider in North America. Its venom is 15 times more toxic than a rattlesnake's! The female black widow is black and shiny and has a bright orange or red marking shaped like an hourglass on her round stomach. While the black widow spider has very toxic venom, it doesn't inject a whole lot when it bites.

Funnel-web Spiders

Size: Up to 2 inches (5 cm) long
Location: Eastern Australia

Funnel-web spiders live along the coast of eastern Australia and have sharp, strong fangs that inject a powerful venom. This group of spiders gets its name from the cone-shaped webs they spin. A bite from a funnel-web spider has been known to kill a person within 15 minutes, but most bites aren't serious.

Leggy Hunters

Spiders only eat meat, so they have to hunt insects and small animals for food. Spiders use venom to knock out their prey but they don't have teeth to tear up and chew meat. So how does a spider chow down? It injects special digestive juices into the prey to break down its body tissues. The prey dissolves, and the spider sucks up its meal!

The Ouch Factor

Most spider bites happen when a person accidentally steps or lies down on a spider that's hiding in a shoe or in bedsheets. The spider bites because it's trapped or surprised. But even if a person gets bit, no spider is so venomous that it could kill someone instantly.

This snake is being milked for its venom.

When people are bitten or stung by a very venomous animal, how do doctors treat them? If the bite or sting is very serious, doctors will give the patient **antivenin** (ANN-tee-VEH-nin) to stop the effects of the venom. Read on to learn more about this life-saving stuff.

MAKING ANTIVENIN

The first step in making antivenin is to catch the venomous animal you're making the antivenin for. Catching the animal isn't always easy—sometimes they're hard to find! Once scientists catch the animal, they "milk" it to get the animal to release its venom. Most animals only inject a drop or two of venom at one time, so scientists have to keep milking the animal until they collect enough.

HORSING AROUND

Once scientists collect enough venom, they inject small amounts of it into big farm animals, like horses. The horses' blood produces chemicals to fight against the venom. Scientists remove these chemicals and use them to make the antivenin. Making antivenin doesn't come cheap—a single dose can cost from $50 to $2,000! But it's worth it, since antivenins have saved thousands of people from deadly bites and stings.

 A special rescue unit is set up in Florida to help venomous snakebite victims. The unit carries many different types of antivenin to help people who have been bitten by some of the world's most venomous animals.

MORE TOXIC CRITTERS

Scorpions, snakes, and spiders are the most famous of the venomous animals, but they aren't the only toxic critters around. Read on to meet a few more dangerous and deadly creatures.

▶ **Poison dart frog**

FLASHY FROGS

Don't let the size of our next critters fool you—their poison packs some serious punch! **Poison dart frogs** are no bigger than your thumb, but a single drop of their poison can kill several adults! These frogs live in the tropical rain forests of South and Central America and they're easy to spot, with their patterns of red, black, yellow, green, or blue.

Poison dart frogs secrete poison from special glands in their skin to protect them from predators. The frogs' bright colors remind predators that they don't taste very good and to stay away. For more info on bright coloring, see page 25.

They really **stand out** in a crowd!

23

▶ **Puss caterpillar**

the skin and release toxins, telling a potential predator to back off! Puss caterpillar stings aren't usually deadly, but they're super-painful.

LeApiN' LizARDS

Only two lizards in the entire world are venomous, and the **Gila** (HEE-luh) **monster** is one of them. Covered in shiny, beaded scales, this lizard can grow up to 20 inches (51 cm) long. A Gila monster uses large, grooved teeth in its lower jaw to chew venom into its prey. Its big, sausage-like tail and body allow it to store fat, so it only needs to eat a few large meals a year.

CAN'T TOuch THiS

This caterpillar might look warm and fuzzy to you, but watch out! This **puss caterpillar** has short spines hidden in its fuzz that are connected to poison sacs. If these spines are touched, they pierce

▶ **Gila monster**

COLOR CODED

Coral snake

Many venomous and poisonous animals are brightly colored to warn predators that they're toxic. Using colors this way is called **aposematism** (ah-POH-seh-MAH-tis-um). While being brightly colored doesn't help a critter hide, it does help a predator remember if eating the animal the first time around was tasty or terrible. By recognizing what the animal looks like, a predator avoids making it a snack again.

Seeing Double

Some sneaky non-toxic animals use aposematism to their advantage. They trick predators into thinking they're poisonous or venomous by copying the colors and patterns of toxic animals. This is known as **mimicry** (MIM-ik-kree).

For example, venomous **coral snakes** have bold stripes of red, black, and yellow to warn predators of their deadly bite. But this is one popular pattern! Over 50 kinds of non-venomous snakes use these stripes—can you tell the difference between this **milk snake** and the coral snake above? Predators can't tell, so they stay away.

Milk snake

The Word Bird

Aposematism is when an animal uses color, sound, or other things to warn other animals not to bother it. *Mimicry* is when an animal copies the way another animal looks or behaves in order to protect itself or get food.

25

UNDER THE SEA

Now that we've met a ton of toxic animals on land, it's time to explore the deep for more dangerous animals. You'll be glad that you aren't an ocean critter!

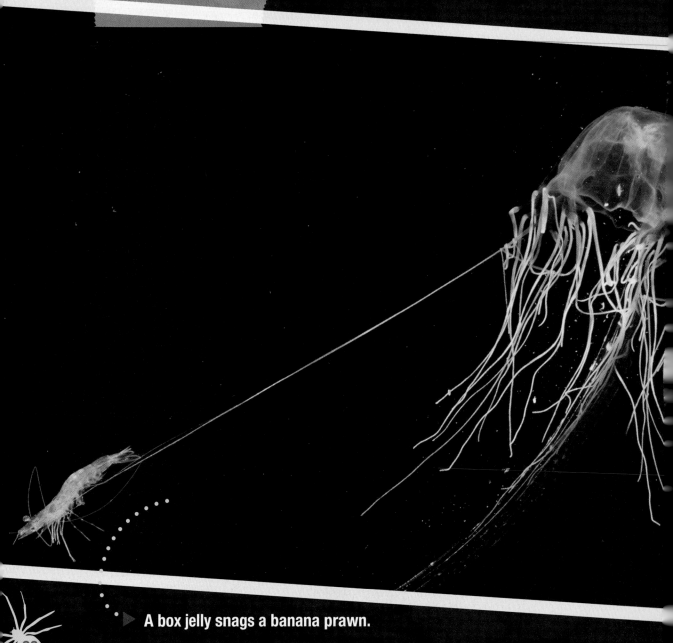

▷ **A box jelly snags a banana prawn.**

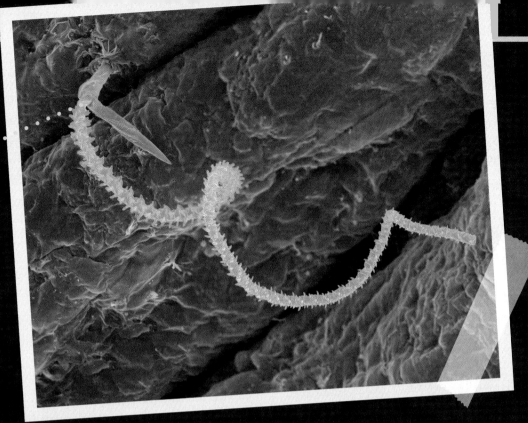

A nematocyst shoots a barb.

Box Jelly

Our next venomous animal might be spineless, but its venom is no joke! **Box jellies** live in the waters of southeast Asia and Australia, and get their name from their cube-shaped bodies.

The largest of the box jellies (also known as the sea wasp) lives off the northeastern coast of Australia in the Great Barrier Reef. And it's a biggie! Its body can grow as large as a basketball, with tentacles up to 15 feet (4½ m) long. At this size, the jelly's tentacles have enough venom to kill three people. During the summer, box jellies hang out in the shallow waters near Australian beaches which makes it super-dangerous for swimmers. In fact, the beaches close down when they find box jellies in the water—better safe than sorry!

Tentacle Tangle

What makes a sea jelly venomous are its **tentacles** (TEN-tuh-kuhls), which it uses to catch food. These tentacles are packed with stinging cells called **nematocysts** (neh-MAT-oh-sists). As a sea jelly floats along, its tentacles trail through the water, trapping fish and other animals. As soon as the prey touches a tentacle, thousands of nematocysts fire and shoot barbs full of toxins into the prey. The toxins stun the prey, and the sea jelly draws it up into its body and makes a meal out of the poor sap. And sea jellies are hard to spot—they're almost invisible underwater!

The Word Bird

A *tentacle* is a long, flexible arm or leg that's used for moving, feeling, or grabbing stuff.

DeaD RingeR

The **blue-ringed octopus** is a fellow Aussie and just as dangerous as the box jelly, although it's much smaller—it's the size of a tennis ball! This octopus gets its name from the bright blue rings that flash on its skin when it's threatened. It hangs out in coral reefs, catching small fish, crabs, and shrimp for dinner. This octopus grabs its prey with its eight flexible arms, and injects a deadly dose of venom using the beak hidden underneath its body.

Something's Fishy

Take a look at the pic below. Believe it or not, that's the world's most venomous fish! **Stonefish** look more like warty fuzz than fish, but all that stuff helps hide it while it's lying on the seafloor waiting for a meal. Stonefish have a dozen spines down their backs that are loaded with toxins. And the spines are super-sharp! People who are stung by stonefish often step on them with their bare feet because they don't see them on the ground. Stonefish stings are serious— without medical treatment, a person can die within a few hours.

Blue-ringed octopus

Stonefish

Lionfish

Stripes 'n' Spines

Lionfish are a group of fish found all over the world that are known for their showy stripes and long spines on their fins. But these beautiful fish are also very venomous! Hidden at the base of each long spine is a venom sac. If an attacker gets poked, the spine shoots a dose of venom into its skin. While the venom isn't deadly, it's powerful stuff. Some kinds of lionfish can knock an adult human out cold!

Venomous? They're not lion!

29

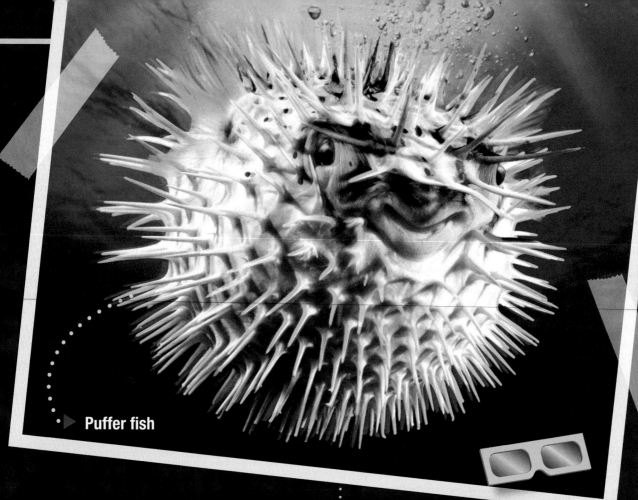

▶ **Puffer fish**

PUFFER POWER

Unlike the two fish on pages 28–29, the **puffer fish** is a poisonous fish that gets its name from an unusual kind of defense. If threatened, the puffer fish sucks in water or air and blows up into a prickly balloon. Although a puffer fish can't make a quick getaway while it's in balloon mode, being a big, spiky ball keeps predators from swallowing it. The last thing any animal wants is a meal that it can choke on!

There's another good reason for predators to stay away from puffer fish. Puffer fish are loaded with

tetrodotoxin, a toxin that's extremely dangerous. This toxin is made by bacteria living inside the fish, and are distributed throughout its body. Like the coral snakes you read about on page 25, puffer fish have spots and patterns that warn other animals that they're toxic, too.

Talk about tox-**sick**!

that's Wild! Although it's poisonous, raw puffer fish is used to make a special dish called *fugu* in Japan. A chef with a special license has to prepare the fish carefully. But even then, people still die every year from puffer fish poisoning.

Q & A WITH HERPETOLOGIST
BILL HOLMSTROM

Meet Bill Holmstrom, a collections manager at the Bronx Zoo in New York City. Bill is a **herpetologist** (her-puh-TAHL-oh-jist), which means that he's an expert on reptiles and amphibians. At the zoo, Bill cares for venomous snakes and Gila monsters, so we asked him a few questions about these amazing animals.

Q: How did you get interested in herpetology?

A: My father liked fish and frogs, and we kept tanks of live animals in our basement when I was a kid. Since the time I was about eight, I was out in the woods collecting animals on my own and spent my free time in the fields, woods, lakes, and streams around my home.

Q: Have you ever been bitten by a venomous animal?

A: No one on staff, including me, has ever been bitten by a venomous reptile. We're very thoroughly trained and are careful to avoid accidents when handling these animals.

Q: Do you have a favorite venomous or poisonous animal?

A: I think the rhinoceros viper is the most beautiful snake, venomous or otherwise. I also have a great respect for and fascination with king cobras, the longest, and perhaps the most intelligent, of the venomous reptiles.

Q: What's an interesting fact about poisonous or venomous reptiles and amphibians?

A: A really interesting fact about these animals is that their toxins, whether in their venom or on their skin, are being used in medicines to help fight diseases, such as cancer.

Q: What's the most important thing that people should remember if they ever come across a venomous snake?

A: Give them plenty of respect and distance. Probably 90 percent of the venomous snakebites in the U.S. happen because people try to kill or handle animals that they don't respect or understand. Snakes aren't interested in attacking, and they only defend themselves if they can't get away. If you leave them alone, they won't bother you.

MORE ACTION-PACKED ADVENTURES COMING SOON!

This has been quite a trip! You've checked out some superb scorpions, sneaked a peek at snakes and spiders, and dove into the deep to see some awesome animals. But there's so much more for us to explore! Join us again next time as we search for more incredible creatures on our next action-packed adventure. See you soon!

▶ **A green lynx spider catches a bee.**